FIVE GOLD RINGS

Joanna Laurens

FIVE GOLD RINGS

OBERON BOOKS
LONDON

First published in this version in 2003 by Oberon Books Ltd.
(incorporating Absolute Classics)
521 Caledonian Road, London N7 9RH
Tel: 020 7607 3637 / Fax: 020 7607 3629

e-mail: oberon.books@btinternet.com
www.oberonbooks.com

ISBN: 1 84002 375 9

Illustration: John McFaul

Printed in Great Britain by Antony Rowe Ltd, Chippenham.

One runs the risk of weeping a little, if one lets himself be tamed.

'Where are the men?' the little prince at last took up the conversation again. 'It is a little lonely in the desert…'

'It is also lonely among men,' the snake said.

The little prince gazed at him for a long time.

'You are a funny animal,' he said at last. 'You are no thicker than a finger…'

'But I am more powerful than the finger of a king,' said the snake.

– Antoine de Saint-Exupéry: *The Little Prince*

I'd like to say thank you to those people who have helped me with this play in various ways. Daragh Carville, Craig Higginson, Katherine Mendelsohn and Michael McKinnie have all provided detailed feedback on the text at different stages of development. Michael Attenborough, St John Donald and Simon Reade have each been instrumental in moving the play from page to stage and realising the first production. The Pearson Trust and the BDI have both provided me with financial support. To all these, thanks.

Characters

HENRY
father to Simon and Daniel

SIMON
Henry's son, Miranda's husband

MIRANDA
Simon's wife

DANIEL
Henry's son, Freja's husband

FREYJA
Daniel's wife

Five Gold Rings was first performed at the Almeida Theatre, London on 11 December 2003, with the following cast:

HENRY, David Calder

SIMON, Will Keen

MIRANDA, Helen McCrory

DANIEL, Damian Lewis

FREYJA, Indira Varma

Director, Michael Attenborough

Designer, Es Devlin

Dramaturg, Katherine Mendelsohn

Lighting, Adam Silverman

Music, Adam Cork

Movement, Jane Gibson

Sound, John Leonard

Scene One

A sundial. The sense of sand, dust; abrasion. Heat haze. HENRY is seated in a chair which is suggestive of a throne. He holds a stick / staff. He audibly taps the following in Morse code: (. . . - - - . . .) (S.O.S.) on the arm of his chair; he does not concentrate on this, the tapping being a nervous tic which is the equivalent of drumming fingers. This Morse code motif perhaps becomes a musical motif that recurs occasionally throughout the play, in a minimalist way.

HENRY holds, clutched in one fist, some creased and folded old letters. On the floor is a Monopoly board, mid-game.

HENRY sits, tapping for a while. Sometimes he thinks he hears noises off, and then he calls out 'Simon?' or 'Daniel?' or 'Hello Simon/Daniel?'. He sits tense, listening, for a few moments, before relaxing when no one enters.

HENRY: Where?
　　Where you, my sons?
　　You left the city yet?
　　You crossing the desert?
　　You in Simon's fast car,
　　looking for food here,
　　looking for father?

Pause.

　　I'm here.
　　But when I'm not/

Pause. HENRY folds the letters up small in his hand and then listens.

　　Simon? Daniel? Simon-Daniel? Hello? Hello my sons, hello?

Enter FREYJA. She is upstage of HENRY, who cannot turn around enough to see her. He tries to get up, shuffles forward in his seat, puts both hands on either side of him and attempts to push up.

Who? Who? Who's there? I/

FREYJA moves around and towards him and kisses him.

FREYJA: Me, Henry. Freyja.

I'm ahead of them. Bringing their presents.
I hitched a ride.
Like last year.

Pause.

HENRY: Ah, Freyja. Hello, hello. Come in, come in.
(*FREYJA is already 'in'.*) Dangerous, hitching.

FREYJA: Not for me. Oh, Happy Christmas. (*Kisses him.*)

HENRY: (*HENRY feels he must stand to wish her the same, so he does, with some effort.*)
Happy Christmas Freyja.

He holds her at arms length and smiles.

It is: hair shorter.
Skin lighter.
Wrists thinner.

Awkward pause.

Where they, my sons?

FREYJA: It's a short-time they'll be here. And Miranda.
It's Daniel has our gift for you.

HENRY: Ah, to me nothing.
To me no one.

Pause.

Where are the secrets for this year? What did you get for
me to give them?

FREYJA: You'll give Simon a jumper
the colour of cherries.
Finest rare wool, with silk woven into the threads.
You'll give Daniel a fountain pen
with gravings etched on the nibb,
and a scottle made of gold.
You'll give Miranda a necklace with a diamond hanging.
You'll give me, a scarf.

HENRY: Just a scarf?

FREYJA: Yes.

Pause.

HENRY: Thank you, Freyja. (*Pause.*)

The only I have to give them is my self.
Children are all 'take, take, take'.
But as I am old,
it is in the interests of economy
for me to give me until my neckskin downhangs
turkeyish, outsized.
It is for them to take me until, slimmed, leaning on only
words, I mumble with my feet.
If I give them enough, perhaps I will pass me over to
them;
buried as a seed, be pushed into life.

Pause.

Well/ There a jar out back, has coins in. Just little spare
ones, you know. I can't/ well/ there's not enough for all
that, you know. Just, maybe, five, towards it?

FREYJA: Henry, no. It's alright.

HENRY begins to fiddle with his pockets, trying to extract as much as he has on him.

FREJYA: Henry.

HENRY: (*Handing her odd assortment of coins.*)
Here. That's two.

FREYJA: (*Rejecting the money.*)
No.

Henry. All the years I'm knowing you, I only want to know why. It's always I've been wanting to know why. Why you've never no money. For buying these every year, please you tell me why. There was a once, there was a onetime you had money?

Pause.

In explanation, HENRY offers her the letters he holds. She takes them.

Reading letters.

Henry,
Why do you send me so much? Are you insane? I don't want it all. I'm returning all but two thousand, which we need until we're settled. You need it to look after the boys. I know you'll do that better than ever I could.
Sarah.

Henry,
You can't buy my love. Please stop this. I don't want to be bought. I don't want your marriage. I don't want you. Stay out of my life. You know I've found someone else.
Sarah.

Henry,
If I accept all this, it is only on the understanding that you will not attempt to contact me again. I don't understand you. Why can't you be bitter like anyone else

would be? I will pay it in tomorrow. I'm returning your letter. Please let me go.
Sarah.

She begins to read the following last letter, but HENRY speaks it from memory. She falls silent and follows the letter as he recites.

HENRY: My Sarah,
A door ajar, the night calls in.
A jar agape, the lid falls off.
Agape love, the purse left loose.
It's all just a matter of give and take.
Of losing virginity and stealing a way.
Yours Henry.

Silence.

Gesturing to letters.

And so there's my nothing.
And now she's but this ink.
She's but this ink.

They always leave, you see. They always leave.

Pause.

FREYJA: I'm sorry, Henry. (*Pause.*) How many years she gone now? Many.

HENRY: Many. Too, too many. But still. She might come back. She knows where I live.

FREYJA: Henry, tell them. Tell Simon-Daniel you have nothing.

HENRY: Never. (*Pause.*) My sons.

He fingers his arm roughly.

Old.

Old knotted-rope pulse.
My pulserope. My boys would have that too;
they see me rich as removed fat,
a Priam cut above the breast.

FREYJA: They see you so rich you make them sick.

HENRY: They see me wrong.

Freyja, I have no money and
they would not love my nothing.
They would leave me if they knew,
and so they will never see the lie until
I die.

They always leave, you see.
Like her, they'd leave like her, they knew my nothing.
But they see me rich, they might stay.
And *I'm* the father. It should be *me, my* pockets
spilling out when I sit down.

Referring to presents.

So thank you.

Pause.

To FREYJA.

Come here.
I might not have much, but

Passing FREYJA his watch.

when I die (not soon, Freyja) but when I die,
Simon, this to him.
This to time his nights, counting the dark.
To give shoutings at seven a.m. and spear him from
sleep.
To Simon, bornfirst son,
this to him.

He takes several photographs from his wallet and caresses
them, pausing over one for each description, before passing
them to FREYJA.

To Daniel, these. These to hold the sappy moments.
To pin us in strange clothes to thick creamy paper,
smashed by foldings and fadings and feelings.
The drinkdregs of parties across time:

My longgone longhair falling out over the middle of a
conversation.

Christmas '71.
A windup mouse.
Simon in boxing gear.

To Daniel, secondborn but equal love,
these to him.

This is all I have worth the giving of.
Freyja, until then they never can get know this nothing.
Never.

FREYJA hands him back the watch and photos.

FREYJA: Never will I say it, Henry.

HENRY: I want them close now. As sand wants water.
Everything will be as it was when they were boys;
here in the desert,
life is

in the name of the farmer
and of the fun and of the holidays.

Our men;
let them stay.

FREYJA: Our men.

Pause.

FREYJA: Henry/ I/ Daniel and I have problems. As his
father, please you talk to him?

*Exit FREYJA with her coat and bag. HENRY resumes
the Morse code tapping under the following.*

HENRY: Simon. Daniel.
Do you know how to craft, do you know how to listen,
do you know how to fight, do you know how to answer,
do you know how to save, do you know how to give up,
do you know how to kill, to slaughter?
I do. That is the waisted fat of the old, buoying me up.
Not your own middleaged spreads.

Where?
Where you, my sons,
come to pass this Christmas
in the desert?

HENRY casts two dice on the Monopoly board.

Scene Two

Later. DANIEL, MIRANDA, and SIMON have just arrived.

*Throughout the play there is a strange tension between DANIEL
and SIMON, carried in looks, in brief touches, in body language
and in pauses. It is certainly competitive, but occasionally there
is another flavour to it, which could be flirtation, in a 'sizing
someone up' kind of way.*

*FREYJA helps with the coats / bags. She watches DANIEL but
stays away from him.*

DANIEL: And there was me, there was, saying right hard,
take you a hard right, Simon

MIRANDA: but Simon was not having nothing of it, he

(DANIEL: he wasn't, no)

MIRANDA: was going on like to moon or

SIMON: yes, it is *my* lateness, is *all* our lateness, sorry sweet
farth. It was the wrong way.

The sky cried down the day
and the mountains crew me come
with their redded sky; come go
over the hills and far away.

Pause.

HENRY: (*Quickly.*)
Coat, give me your coat Simon.
And Miranda, Miranda, you stop the door;
there's incoming sand.
Why only once a year, only once a year you're here?
SimonDaniel, now is a fullhouse here.
You in your old rooms,
like when you little were.
Just like then, just like then

To himself.
(only without her)

DANIEL: (*Quickly.*)
Ten days, ten days we with you, farth.

We all came out to get away.
To be here in the desert.
I came to find my wooden hobby-horse.
I came to find my yellow truck.
I came to find the story Simon-I wrote
and buried under the garden fence.

Pause. Exit HENRY with coats.

FREYJA: (*To SIMON and DANIEL.*)
Tell him. Now!

MIRANDA: Is for him to know.

FREYJA: Tell him.

MIRANDA: He must leave here.

Pause.

DANIEL: (*To SIMON.*)
You're the eldest.

Enter HENRY.

FREYJA: (*Discovering Monopoly game.*)
Henry. This last year's game?

HENRY: Yes/ I/
You all went off away across the dark to city lights. And
I was trying to put it away, I was trying Freyja, but when
I looked to it, it said youse to me – that big red hotel
was saying of the time when Daniel tipped coffee on
him, and the hotel had got to be wiped, yes it had. And
Miranda's boat in gaol there was saying of when the
phone rang, and then went you all to answer it, and
jumped on each other, and then you landed, you landed,
you landed all in a pile but Miranda got the phone, and
then you put Miranda in gaol like to punish her, like to
say all-*we* is wanting the phone.

All laugh.

And then you went.
And then you weren't here no more.

Pause.

Only there was a smudge of you left.
In the way you last left the cards lying.
In the smell of Simon's aftershave on King's Cross.
In the sticky jam on Daniel's Scottie dog.
So I left it out the year. Only but just dusted it.
And now we can finish it.
Now.

Pause.

Why must always you be straining
back to the city,
dogs on a leash?

Pause.

Max, big bull Max:
the two-you used to ride him when you were small.
He died, it was six months it was he died.
Dropped himself dead on the sand.
And you weren't here no more.
Didn't see that now, did you,
didn't see big bull Max
kiss himself down the earth?

Pause.

(DANIEL: Come to the city with us, farth.
    Then we will be in your life.)

HENRY: (*Ignoring DANIEL.*)
    And was hurting him to die, was.
    So I sat to him, said;
    'Big bull Max, mine,
    I'm here.' (*Pause.*)
    And then was I, with a hand to his neck.
    And *then* was I hearing:
    When his voice ploughed the clouds,
    when his song wrung out
    and sowed the sky
    with blood and love.

    I was here.

    Silence.

SIMON: Come you to the city with us, farth.

MIRANDA: Sleep childclose to us.

19

HENRY: (*Awkward, embarrassed.*)
Never.
This is where
This is where I lived
This is where I lived with
her.

SIMON: We just put our bags in our rooms, farth.

Exit SIMON, DANIEL and FREYJA. MIRANDA moves to exit, but HENRY catches hold of her arm.

HENRY: This is where I lived with her, Miranda.

Patting his pocket with the letters in.

And now she's but this ink, she's but this ink, she's but this ink.

Releasing MIRANDA's arm.

Not that it's ever *you're* knowing what it is to be with only *one* other,
over and across the days.

MIRANDA: What?

HENRY looks uncomfortable.

What?

HENRY: What you told me last year. You were drunk.

MIRANDA: Ten years. Ten years back, Henry. Before Simon. You know I was poor. You know I was. You know. Leave it.

HENRY: Sorry, Miranda. Sorry.

SIMON: (*Off – calling.*)
Miranda, sweet?

Exit MIRANDA.

HENRY: (*To himself.*)

Was my go, was my go anyway.

HENRY looks at the dice he threw on the board earlier and moves his playing piece, the 'old boot', around the board.

Calling.

It's your turn!

Pause.

It's your turn!

Pause.

It's your turn!

Pause. He takes the screwed up letters from his hand and unfolds them. He feels the paper with his fingers, rubs it against his cheek, smells it. He licks the used seal of the envelope. As a cat with cat-nip. Strangely passionate for an old man.

There was a woman, I loved her.
There was a woman, I loved her.
There is a woman, I love her.
Still.
As weed out of water.

Silence.

DANIEL: (*Off.*) Father?

HENRY hides the letters under the sundial. He cannot move very fast and is flustered and slightly out of breath when DANIEL enters. Enter DANIEL with blood smeared on his neck.

DANIEL: Farth, have you a plaster?

Enter MIRANDA.

MIRANDA: And I need some soap.

DANIEL: Cut myself shaving.
    The blooding won't stop.
    Is my throat crying out.

MIRANDA: Dirt from driving.
    The blackening of the city
    in my hands, dark palms.

HENRY: Yes, my Daniel. It is/ There is/ Miranda, I have
    some. I think.

    Exit HENRY.

Scene Three

Silence.

DANIEL: No more the city.

    Cool quiet now.

    Bleat of the frog under the cold stone.
    Turned over and folded under in earth.
    Even song of the fly is sanctified;
    is cool quiet now.

    Silence.

MIRANDA: Daniel. You-Freyja seem far apart. (*Pause.*)
    Why?

    Silence. DANIEL puts his head in his hands.

    Daniel?

    Pause.

DANIEL: There was a once, there was a onetime did I love
    her.
    Both-we woked with pillowcrease faces
    and said on each other
    you look lovely.

Pause, then, as a parent to a child; in a singing voice.
All gone.

Lost is the time of whispered worlds,
the pushing through hairs across nights.
Lost is the ricochet of (loveyou, loveyou).
The pitching of skin in song.

How to tell her?
Next her at nights I cry salt whorls into my ears,
solitary snailshelled liquid sadness.
Secret as a boy covers a birthmark,
going swimming with his friends.

But still I have known her.
But still she has known me.

And there's no hiding this here.
No more the city.

Bark of the dog gnawing his hard bone.
Turned over and folded under in earth.
Even song of the fly is sanctified;
is cool quiet now.

Is cool quiet now.

Pause. MIRANDA approaches DANIEL as though to comfort him. Enter FREYJA. MIRANDA immediately stops and redirects this movement.

FREYJA: Dan? You must tell.

Pause. DANIEL starts, scared.

The water. Tell Henry. (*Pause.*) How the water for the house soon is

DANIEL: gone.

Pause.

FREYJA: The water

MIRANDA: heavying his earth has

FREYJA: left. (*Pause.*)
Trailing last wetdrabs through the ground,

DANIEL: like blunt sweated fingerends dragging shapes on
my back.

MIRANDA: The water in the river

FREYJA: has cried itself

DANIEL: out. (*Pause.*)
A childvoice thrown against the night.

Pause.

Freyja. What'll we say?

FREYJA: We'll talk the truth:
He can't live here no more,
only but must come back to the city
with us.

Pause.

DANIEL: He will be broken.

Pause. FREYJA approaches DANIEL.

MIRANDA: He is rich. He will break even. (*Pause – she sees
FREYJA approaching.*)

Dan, is it *still* your neck is bleeding?

*Flirting FREYJA takes DANIEL's suit jacket from him
and throws it down. DANIEL remains rigid throughout.*

FREYJA: Miranda, I think Henry wants you.

To DANIEL.

Moon, highfliermine.
Take off your clothes
and let me follow suit.

MIRANDA: Dan, I am to get Henry now. With your
plaster. To stop it.

DANIEL: He will be back soon. Stay, Miranda.

Pause.

MIRANDA: Freyja is right; you must talk the truth.

Exit MIRANDA.

DANIEL: (*To MIRANDA.*)
To Henry, yes? To Henry, Miranda, you mean?

FREYJA: Recall our caving trip.

(DANIEL: over four years now)

FREYJA: You me Miranda, a three party affair.
(Simon couldn't come.)
We were married two months later.
Was a teasy wind thwacking
cables on openair liftsides.
But we never got to rockbottom
as the lift slamstop jerked
and you downed me, deliberately.
I snatched at your shorts but slipped.
From the floor of the lift
I tried to admire the granite boulders,
the graphite, the streaks of quartz in the cliffs –
I saw your shoestring was trailing.
But it was hard, because
your shorts were kneed,
revealing skyblue undies
asking 'why' in 3D.

DANIEL: (*Bitterly.*) For god's sake/

FREYJA: /And you fingered for us the white slice
of moon, hooking the sky.

DANIEL: Freyja. This isn't working. Father is to bring a
plaster here.

FREYJA: Daniel, fullbodied,
  I'll lay you quick as a tablefortwo.

DANIEL: Any minute he is to bring a plaster here.

FREYJA: Daniel, highskyer, fingering the barbed C of the
  moon,
  you caught me.

  The curl in the air,
  the string of your shoe,
  the de-elevator;
  I fell for you hook, line and sinker.

  *Enter HENRY holding plaster and soap and MIRANDA
  carrying a transparent basin of water. DANIEL has his
  back to them and does not realise they are there.*

DANIEL: Freyja.
  There's no point in you
  lying like a wishbone,
  always lowering the looped horns of
  your youandus uterus at me;
  legs open, for a man
  soft as cheese!

FREYJA: (*To HENRY.*)
  Please talk to him.

  Exit FREYJA.

DANIEL: (*To HENRY.*) I can't, farth. I can't anymore so
  Freyja-me are breaking up.
  There's nothing between us.
  Waking this morning to freshlysqueezed birdsong
  under a sheet of cloud, I rolled over to find
  the other person had cleared.
  This the love that flesh is air to.

  Pause.

HENRY: Plaster?

> *DANIEL takes the plaster and the basin of water.*
> Anything you want, anything you want just ask.
> Is like to be without skin,
> to be without the person you love.

> *HENRY hands the soap to MIRANDA.*
> (*To DANIEL.*)
> I know/ I know that you Freyja/
> I know.
> Freyja told me.
> Is raw, is like to be without skin,
> to be without the person you love.

> We will talk.

> *Exit HENRY.*

Scene Four

MIRANDA moves forward and places a hand on DANIEL's shoulder. DANIEL realises she overheard his 'confession' and is embarrassed she will think him impotent. He puts his hand on hers for a moment. As DANIEL bathes his neck, the water turns an exaggeratedly deep red. He finishes.

DANIEL: Miranda.
 I fib.
 I fib to Freyja.
 I fib to farth.

 There is nothing wrong with me
 but lack of love for her,
 but lack of lust for her.

MIRANDA: Nothing?

DANIEL: Nothing.
 I lie to her. But not on her.

Sing-song, mocking, bitter.

Liar, liar, my pants is on fire.
She sings my stick asleep.
I claim impotence absolves me.

MIRANDA: I'm sorry, Daniel.

DANIEL: (*Bitter, joking in embarrassment.*)
It's a hard time for me.

He laughs. Silence.

MIRANDA: (*Indicating the plaster.*)
Shall I…?

*DANIEL smiles, nods and inclines his head. MIRANDA
sticks the plaster on his neck.*

MIRANDA: Say to me how it was when you were little
here Dan? You, Simon, Henry?

DANIEL: Everything was of gold then.
The sand, the sun.
And in the backing was the mountains,
green taps on the shoulder saying
I'm here.

MIRANDA: I'm here.

Pause.

DANIEL: Now only can there be life while there's a well.
Will be gone soon.
Was a river before. Fish.
Now the river's gone. The fish dead.
When first it happened Simon-I/ (*Pause.*)

Has he ever said anything?

MIRANDA: What?

DANIEL: Simon. Has he ever said anything?

MIRANDA: About what?

Pause.

DANIEL: We/ I/ were twelve and/ (*Pause.*)

MIRANDA: Daniel?

DANIEL: Simon-I laughed,
    slung fish at each other,
    danced brotherlove on their bodies.
    But when they weren't coming back
    we were sad and lay on golden stomachs
    making fish noises, singing water burburs
    for hours.

    And if you layed on the sand, loggy,
    and if you put your breath out like a sheet over the gold,
    you would see snakes move past;
    whips cut off at the hand.

    We rode bareback.
    We danced when it rained.
    We read each other's bodies,
    changing like the wind.

    We made six secret societies
    where we were the only members.
    We ate a mouse Simon caught.
    Raw, like cats.

    We could make a door.
    We could skin a rabbit.
    We could make fire.

    We knew the way to walk sideways up to a cat giving
    birth.
    We knew that a woman bleeds every twenty-eight days.
    We could tell the time by the sun.
    We couldn't write.
    The password to the barn was
    mum.

Pause.

We never knew her. She left when we were small.

MIRANDA: How is it that she could?

DANIEL: She met a man. It's not all you women want children.

MIRANDA: Daniel,
   I have the want for a child,
   a want what stealt its way
   with me, like a cool hand
   in a park
   up a tunic
   during a break time.
   I have no say in it.
   I have the want of a child.

   And in a whole year of wanting,
   Simon never said he'd taken the shortcut,
   never told me he'd had the snip
   until last week.

DANIEL: (*Disbelief.*)
   No.

MIRANDA: Before that
   he said it was
   God,
   the boy with his finger in the dyke.

DANIEL: (*Pause, then to himself.*)
   Simple Simon.

   To MIRANDA.

He didn't tell me, Miranda. Never did he tell me.

MIRANDA: Why did he…?

DANIEL: He thinks it was him-me, split our parents up.

MIRANDA: He won't have children so as to *stay* with me?

DANIEL: Yes.

DANIEL moves to comfort MIRANDA.

MIRANDA: But Daniel.
In the city. Every day I dream.
Lie alone under coarse pink blanket cornered in silk, I do.
Feet more feeling;
more nerves; more nervous
to the touch of a bit of rough.
Push hands up under sheets and
make a baby
of them.

In the city. Every day I dream.
Of, standing by a lake,
woman and child
in a foxglove light.
Winged dirt insects shake
off night, pad silent,
skate the thick
inabsorbent
muscle of the lake.
She's dressed to kill
in briefs and smalls.
The child spooning her breast into his mouth,
(Madonna, my dinner).

An affair of air.

Lie low under coarse pink blanket cornered in silk, I do,
taking the rough with the smooth.
The tick of my feet
marking the cover right
up to the sky.

Lie by myself

DANIEL: I do.
  Lie with myself

MIRANDA: I do.
  Lie to myself

DANIEL: I do.

Silence. They kiss. MIRANDA pulls away.

DANIEL: Sorry. I/

Noise off. Enter SIMON. MIRANDA and DANIEL stare at SIMON. Pause.

SIMON: What? Where's the soap? Miranda?

Exit DANIEL.

Scene Five

SIMON: Is it Freyja you been talking him about? Leave that alone. Something is wrong there. Like what farth used to say; picking at things is only making them bleed. I can see it. Soap?

Pause. MIRANDA hands him the soap.

Hungry?

MIRANDA shakes her head. SIMON tries to kiss MIRANDA. She turns away. SIMON busies himself with something.

Thirsty?

MIRANDA is silent. SIMON again tries to put his arm around MIRANDA. She allows him but turns away.

Miranda. Please, not again. I'm sorry.

Referring to his groin.

Tying the knot means nothing.
You me – still the same.

MIRANDA: (*Referring to her wedding ring.*)
>Tying the knot means everything.
>I want a child.
>Waster.
>I'm notwanting your seedless passion.

SIMON removes his arm and retreats. He is shaken and scared.

SIMON: Miranda,
>before I found you I was a rich single liver,
>up three thinrailed flights of hard linoleum.

MIRANDA: (*Mocking.*)
>Meat and two veg for one, small saucepanned,
>boilinthebag life.
>Calor gas. Burner. Blue flame. Red steak.
>Thin slither of yellowness melting?

SIMON: Yes.
>Worked nine to eight.
>Office.
>All tied up, it suited me down to the ground.
>Listened to plain-chant on headphones.

MIRANDA: Then I founded you.

SIMON: Remember,
>you were in constant kissfits that night,
>a boobytrap to die for with arms
>which folded like cream.
>I was instant as the coffee and biscuits.
>My head over your heels; a licence to feel.
>To fondle, fiddle, fist, fornicate and fuck you allfoured.

>Your breath.
>Straight as a blue note.
>And below,
>the caved tang of your crowd
>closing for the kill.

You took me
back to basics.

Silence.

I think/ I know I was your first.

MIRANDA:
(*Angry.*) What would you been, our child?
You would have pissed black oil.
You would have shat clear diamonds.
Your bright first words would have soliddropped around
your feet for birds to steal.

Our conditional child.

Silence.

To SIMON.

And now your line's gone dead.
Simon, my source,
you cut me off.

SIMON: Useless juiceless S bend,
the vas deferens.
Curled skinlets floored
at the barber surgeons.

MIRANDA: Was it a cutandgo job?

SIMON: Miranda. Stop.
I won't take a chance.
Children.
Split you apart like Daniel-I done on mumdad,
softly broached them with those babylonglegs.
To me you wired are, little hotline;
we're coupled poletopole.
Here in the desert
in the dark
in love.

We all whip out bad parts.
My mother removed my father.
They gotiton, they haditoff.
They had it out after she'd had us out
with a forcep twuck.
And, babied, we her sides rode;
our chobbielegs saltyglobes to her sweating flanks.
No wonder she threw us off, our mum.
The revolution of marriage.
The giveandtake,
gostraighttogaol,
winorlose of it all.

We all cut out the bad parts.
(*Sung.*) All gone.

Pause.

Scene Six

FREYJA with SIMON's keys, DANIEL trying to catch her. Noise and excitement – a lack of control. HENRY does not raise his voice.

DANIEL: Simon, she's the keys.

FREYJA positions herself so HENRY's chair is between them.

HENRY: A drink, who's wanting a drink? A topup? Daniel?

DANIEL: Simon, get her.

SIMON joins DANIEL in trying to catch FREYJA.

HENRY: Simon, can I get you a drink? Is anyone still hungry? Food's in the kitchen.

SIMON almost catches FREYJA. She drops the keys. SIMON passes them to DANIEL.

SIMON: Dan!

DANIEL gives the keys to MIRANDA.

DANIEL: Alright, that's enough. Let's play Monopoly.

SIMON pours himself a drink.

SIMON: Whose go, farth?

HENRY: (*Not hearing.*)
What?

SIMON: Whose go is it?

HENRY: I/ well/ I/ was it/

DANIEL: /Mine after farth's.
But look where he's come down.
Park Lane.
Mine.

SIMON: (*To HENRY.*)
Dan's.

MIRANDA: (*To DANIEL.*)
Yours.

FREYJA: (*To HENRY.*)
His.

DANIEL: (*Reading card.*)
Thirty-five.

HENRY: (*Deliberately offering more.*)
Fifty?

SIMON: Dad!

DANIEL: No, Dad.

HENRY continues to hold the money out to DANIEL.

HENRY: Come on.

HENRY takes another fifty and gives it to SIMON, who accepts it, surprised.

Fair's fair.

DANIEL takes the fifty pounds and takes his turn, rolling the dice straightaway.

MIRANDA: Daniel.
Fair as a merry-go-round,
two crown-and-anchor stalls
and a shooting gallery.

Offering DANIEL a card.

Take a chance.

SIMON: (*Mocking, taking her hand, kissing it.*)
Miranda.
Fair as May sunshine on wishingwell gold;
looking up
I am in ore of you.

Laughter. MIRANDA removes his hand.

Referring to the playing-piece.

My car will drive him round the bend.
You'll see.

DANIEL: Yes?

SIMON: Yes. Afterall I *do* work for the industry.

DANIEL: Behind a desk, not a steering wheel.

FREYJA: Shut up or I'll bang your heads together.

MIRANDA: Simon doesn't have one to bang.

All laugh – too suddenly. SIMON throws an arm around MIRANDA.

Who owns Regent Street?

DANIEL: I do. Who owns Oxford Street?

MIRANDA: I do. Who owns Bond Street?

DANIEL: I do.

All laugh.

SIMON: Farth. Every night, we could play this every night, you living in the city.

Silence.

HENRY: Never. Never am I living in the city, Simon. All you can live here though.

Pause.

DANIEL: Farth. We were not wanting to tell you. But.
Is your well run dry.
Is your waterstore passed away.

Silence.

HENRY: All?

SIMON: Yes.

Silence.

HENRY: All?

DANIEL: Yes.

Silence.

HENRY: Gone as is the river is gone?

Silence.

HENRY: Gone as is she is gone?

Pause.

As earlier – singing as a parent to a child.

All gone.

River.
Talk, talk the sundust in your air.
You spoke about the stops of stones.
You licked out the mouths of whelks.
You ran under the thrum of bees
boldbattering on the breakins of buds.

River.
Talk, talk the sundust in your air.
You ground your hips to make flour,
mills spilling piecemeal on the sand.
I sat and saw your cable
passing over the land.

But is all askings to ashes,
but is all dearest to dust.
So did she leave me.
As a fag drops grey
(as an Empire dies out)
as a child grows old;
as iron to rust.

River, boyracer. Don't leave me.

FREYJA: Is already gone, Henry.

*'Here-we-go-again' glances are exchanged during the
following.*

HENRY: Simon, Daniel.
I worked in the telegraph office at your age.
The rimshots of dots,
the brushes of dashes,
the pulsings and beatings
of shared private feelings
passing stopstart/

DANIEL: /Father, Freyja-me should/

SIMON: /We really all should turn in/

HENRY continues and does not appear to have heard DANIEL. His legs are crossed and he rotates his ankle as he speaks.

HENRY: /There was this time.
    The end of a day.
    Mr Gates said to come see him.
    Gates only wanted to say did I know; the first telegram
    picked from magnetic fields
    was the question.

SIMON / DANIEL: 'What hath God wrought?'?

SIMON: (*Aside.*)
    Old man repeats the story
    for the multipath effect of it.

DANIEL: (*Aside.*)
    Old man repeats the story
    while his balled footstop circles carpet.

SIMON: What hath God wrought?

HENRY: (*Looking up now to SIMON – a challenge – this should have the feel of a family 'game'.*)
    …what hath God wrought?

Pause.

    Hmm? Well? From the point of view of a man in the car business, what hath God wrought?

HENRY nods approvingly during the following.

SIMON: Clutch reservoirs.
    Float chambers.
    (Grab throttles.)
    Internal combustion, connecting rods,
    and a little rotary motion, rotary motion, rotary motion,
    to the crankshaft, the camshaft.
    Forced-oil lubrication.

(Flywheel, spent gases; fanbelt.)
The overflow duct, the transfer port, the cylinder.
Alternators, spade connectors.
In the forward drive of thermal to mechanical
metamorphoses,
God hath wrought the Wankel engine.

HENRY: Yes, exactly! Well said.

The same challenge to DANIEL.

What hath God wrought?

DANIEL: What hath God wrought?

HENRY: Yes, from the point of view of a man who's
   followed his father into communications, tell us, what
   hath God wrought?

DANIEL: Softiron cones.
   Duplex.
   (Perfected in Germany, making it possible for one wire
   to permit simultaneous emissions, spontaneous
   fluctuations, erroneous permutations, self-indulgent
   perambulations.)
   The member rotating, the member rotating, the member
   rotating
   inside the communicator
   is driven by a crank pushed by the operator.
   Transmitters and receivers,
   transformers and decepticons.
   All sources of heat emit thermal noise and interference
   resulting in misroarings, misreadings.
   This is the hothouse that God wrought.

MIRANDA: Always this game.

HENRY: You say the well will dry.
   Never am I leaving.
   She might come back.

Silence.

SIMON: (*Offering the dice.*)
  Whose turn?

*DANIEL claims the dice, shakes them, smiling at
MIRANDA. MIRANDA returns his smile.*

DANIEL: Stop.
  A little shot in the dark,
  a mini drive at the Park,
  I want a full set to build there.
  Simon, can I buy your Mayfair?

SIMON: No.

Pause.

DANIEL: (*To SIMON.*)
  You're right –

  To HENRY.

  we should go to bed.
  I/ Good night.

  Exit DANIEL.

HENRY: Stay longer.
  I have doughnuts,

  Exit MIRANDA.

FREYJA: we really

HENRY: almond cakes and. Just ten minutes more?

SIMON: I'll be seeing you morning time. You know. Farth.
  We're not far away.

HENRY: I/ Yes. Yes, my Simon.
  My two sons, my two sons going up in the world.

Scene Seven

Later – night. Outside. The sense of an endless landscape. Two people (DANIEL and MIRANDA.) fall apart. They are naked but their bodies are wet so the sand clings to them – they are almost clothed by sand. Their clothes lie scattered around them. Silence.

MIRANDA: Daniel.

> *Shyness.*

> We could take the car.

DANIEL: I'd drive you wild.

> *Slight laughter. Silence. Shyness.*

> Miranda. (*Pause; shyness.*)

> The ground is smooth in the field tonight.
> Slowly easing off the quicks of your nails
> you pulled sweeping curves
> of flasked water
> pisswarm over nude feet.

He looks to MIRANDA – i.e. will you play? MIRANDA touches his hair.

MIRANDA: The ground is smooth in the field tonight.
Fingering copper coins, the loosechange
of yourself in your pocket,
I saw you partway between cows and chrysanthemums,
between butchers and gardeners.

DANIEL: The ground is smooth in the field tonight.
Whacking off the ears of long grass
you caught the summer sun,
applauded by a magpie's smashing
front stroke against the sky.

MIRANDA: And, before we touched lips,
　　I caught a thrusting of your breath
　　lengthening in the air,
　　like the viewing station of an orgasm.

DANIEL: The ground is smooth in the field tonight.
　　Touching up the chrome on your Chrysler,
　　the heat turned us golden;
　　the continuous tone of a successful connection.

They kiss. MIRANDA takes DANIEL's hand and puts it to her stomach. Pause.

MIRANDA: Imagine, maybe, Daniel.
　　I'll catch the son off you.

Excited silence. As DANIEL speaks, they remove each other's rings.

DANIEL: We must walk away from our old rings
　　and leave them untouched, unanswered,
　　making nuisance calls to our naked hands
　　through dark night lines.

They throw their rings onto the sand.

Let those gold band widths loop there,

MIRANDA: let them lie there,

DANIEL: stopped dead on the sand.

Pause.

MIRANDA: The river might be gone but
　　it rains in me

DANIEL: it rains in me

MIRANDA: it rains in me

DANIEL: intuitively

MIRANDA: into the sea

DANIEL: into the sea

MIRANDA: into the sea

DANIEL: intimacy

MIRANDA: intimacy

DANIEL: intimacy

Pause. He holds her closely.

Flirting.

Miranda.
See what your name does to the register of my
instrument.
Sends it haywire. Springs it skyhigh.

Pause.

Let's leave tomorrow.
You bring the car.

MIRANDA: You bring some money.

DANIEL: Farth is loaded.

It'll be but only a gesture to him.
The potency of my 'impotence'.

He takes a scrap of paper from his pockets and a pencil.
There is a drawing of MIRANDA on one side of the paper.
He writes a few lines on the back. He gives this to
MIRANDA.

Here.
This is my thought of you noclothed
before the day it all came together.

MIRANDA turns the note / drawing over.

MIRANDA: (*Reading the back.*)
To my Miranda. I give you back to you. Love Daniel.

A light is turned on – FREYJA, looking for DANIEL.

FREYJA: (*Off – quietly shouting.*)
Daniel?

They replace their wedding rings and hurriedly throw their clothes on.

DANIEL: You haven't seen me.

DANIEL kisses MIRANDA.

Exit DANIEL. MIRANDA tries to hide the note / drawing in her clothes somewhere.

Scene Eight

Enter FREYJA. Pause. She sees the disturbed sand and MIRANDA looking dishevelled and sandy.

FREYJA: Where's Daniel?

Silence.

Where's Daniel?

MIRANDA: I haven't seen him. Couldn't sleep.

Silence.

FREYJA: Miranda, since we got here/

FREYJA sees the note / drawing which MIRANDA has. She snatches it from her.

To/
To my Miranda. I give you back to you. Love/
Daniel.

MIRANDA: Sorry, sorry.

Silence.

FREYJA: But I love him.
But I love him.

Pause.

Miranda.

But still I have known him.
But still he has known me.

This morning
I woke and he slept on.
I saw the curling of his fingers
his eyelashes
and the way the quick
of his index finger lay white
and fluttered in his breath.
And the sheet lay sighing
between us
and I couldn't touch him with my foot.
When I woke and he slept on
I spent twenty minutes counting
the whorls on his thumb
(fifty-one)
and wondered why it rained in me.
When I woke and he slept on
I knew I would never tell him of
how I woke and he slept on.

I love him. Only I love him.
Henry said he would talk to him about/

MIRANDA: Sorry, Freyja.

There's nothing wrong with him
but lack of love for you,
but lack of lust for you.
You sing his stick asleep
and impotence absolves him.

We're leaving together. For the mountains.

FREYJA: Never.

MIRANDA: Henry is to give him the money we need. It's nothing to him.

Silence.

FREYJA: Miranda. Henry has no money. Look under the sundial. Never are you-Daniel going.

Exit FREYJA with note/drawing.

MIRANDA: No. No. Henry, he is rich. Henry. He is rich. Henry.

He is rich.

Pause.

But/
If she's right/
Henry. Liar.
Where your mermaid's purse,
your packet?
How can you pay Daniel?

Black.

Exit MIRANDA.

Scene Nine

Morning. DANIEL and HENRY – DANIEL is eating an apple.

HENRY: So, what do you have to tell me?

Pause.

DANIEL: Fathermine, to tell you I have/
I have this Braeburn apple,
stealed from your fruit bowl.
And it tells 'you' to me, because when I was small,
you gived me one and sayed
'do you be perfect,' like to say
'do you move here, mountains'.

48

And, holding it now, I look to the mountains to see
are they nearer?

HENRY: No nearer.

Pause.

DANIEL: Fathermine, thankyou much for having this
gettogether.

Pause.

Farth. Please may I borrow some money, please?

Pause. HENRY tries to hide his reaction to this request.

Remember the old Sunday mealtimes;
our cheeky family mouthing off, arguing;
passing the sauce around.
You in charge, carving joints, shouting
'no more of your lip'.
You cut crackling equally,
laying down the lines,
conducting the noise by making
silly snipmaps for us and asking
'who wants my fat?'.

You then said that if there a/ If there's a thing I need but
couldn't, but can't get a loan, to ask you. So I ask you.
You know I/ You know, you know. There's a doctorman,
a medicineman, a specialist. He can fix me up. I'm
broke. I need/ Ten thousand.

Pause. He takes a further bite of the apple.

You'll say wait and see. Pray.
But I'm fed up with wait-watching.
I've asked at communion,
I've taken the host in my mouth.
But for me nothing.
But for me no urge.

You want grandchildren,
so let's put our heads together.
Fathermine, with your lifeline,
have interest.

I know you won't let me down.

HENRY: Daniel. Of course, of course. You will have the
money. It is one of the pleasures of wealth that you can
support those you love. Did you doubt, did you think me
an old miser, eh, eh?

DANIEL: I will make it up to you.

*HENRY takes his cheque book and writes a cheque. His
cheque book is much bigger than a conventional cheque
book.*

HENRY: Daniel. It's not a beggar *you* are.
In the city, when it rains,
I imagine homeless hands are
offered to the citysky,
nailed to the night by stars.
When it rains these crosslegged charmers
of passersby
cry
quiet things

DANIEL: (*Semi-audible.*)
Amen.

HENRY: (*Handing DANIEL the cheque.*)
and take a coin in their mouths.

(DANIEL: The body of Christ.)

HENRY: Do you love me, Daniel?
Do you love me more than your mother?

DANIEL: (*Reaching forward to put a hand on HENRY's knee.*)
I love you more than Simon.

HENRY: Then never you be one of those homeless. You must pay me back. With interest. With interest, Daniel.

Pause. Then HENRY tries to sound casual:

Well, when, you tell me, when are you to pay it in?

DANIEL: Tomorrow. Don't want to lose it, do I Farth?

HENRY: No. No. Now no more. A drink? A little pickmeup perhaps?

DANIEL: No, no fathermine.
I'm fine.

HENRY: (*Gesturing towards Monopoly game.*)
Where are the others; they should come and finish what they've started.

Exit HENRY. Pause.

DANIEL: Sorry. Sorry. You my dad.
There is in me that I'm
not liking to lie on you.
But you are rich and strong.
When I was small, you holded me.
I felt the golden muscles stipple under your shirt
and I knowed there then
that you hold me hardly, in arms.

Enter MIRANDA.

Quiet. Come here.
I have the money.
It was nothing to him.

Pause.

MIRANDA: You/ How?

DANIEL: A fifty for the bus, please farth;
A single journey.

Miranda. If you love me,
let's go.
Mountains minted greenwhite,

MIRANDA: lines of snow calling us high.

DANIEL: Warmed curves,

MIRANDA: suckling the sky.

Exit DANIEL.

*MIRANDA crosses to sundial and finds HENRY's letters.
She reads the first three in silence, the last aloud.*

Reading.

A door ajar, the night calls in.
A jar agape, the lid falls off.
Agape love, the purse left loose.
It's all just a matter of give and take.
Of losing virginity and stealing a way.

Pause.

Old letters, old love, leering at him.
He's not wanting Dan to know his nothing.
So I'll say nothing.
Except to Henry.
Except to him, except to him, except to him.

*She replaces the letters underneath the sundial. Exit
MIRANDA.*

Scene Ten

Enter HENRY with the note / drawing.

HENRY: (*To himself, wondering.*)
This/
This in my room.

Shouting.

Who put this in my room? Freyja?

He turns the drawing over and reads the back.

To my Miranda. I give you back to you. Love Daniel.

Daniel. Daniel and Miranda.

(*Angry.*) Daniel.

Liar. You're not to have her, Daniel. You're not to have her: Fair's fair, poor Simon. Fair's fair.

He thinks.

And you tell me you need a doctor? You're with Miranda, it's never no doctor *you're* needing. (*Beat.*) Miranda/ She's just like her, isn't she? She's just like her. (*Beat.*) But what is it that Dan's needing the money for, then?

He thinks. He finds no answer.

It's *me* the one who's broke. Tomorrow he'll find I have nothing. Tomorrow he'll pay it in. They never can get know my nothing. Never. Is nice to be the giver, is. Is nice to be the giver. Every man is a friend to him that gives. Who is the father here? What sort of father can't provide, eh?

HENRY sits down, pauses, stands up, pauses, sits down again. He seems to be whispering / muttering to himself. He thinks, whilst doing some sort of repetitive auto-erotic contact – i.e. – stroking his thinning hair, rocking slightly, et cetera. Whilst doing this, something occurs to him which frightens him.

Out of his whispers come a shout.

No! Never! Daniel must have his money. But, fair's fair: He won't have Miranda. Poor Simon.

Pause.

Ah. Ah. Simon, Simon, *he* has money/

Beat.

But/ Is this fair? Is this fair, now? (*Beat – he thinks.*) Yes:

To Simon, bornfirst son,
his wife back.
The price: His money.

To Daniel, secondborn but equal love,
the money he wants.
The price: Miranda.

HENRY is pleased with himself.

(*Shouting.*) Simon! Simon?

Enter SIMON with food and drink on a tray. HENRY quickly puts the note / drawing in his pocket. He takes the tray from SIMON.

SIMON: Mind it is you are not spilling it. Watch!

HENRY: I am old and foolish but can still make tea.
Doughnuts and almond cakes and whipped cream and cheese sandwiches

He looks at SIMON for a line.

SIMON: ham sandwiches

HENRY: And ham sandwiches.

SIMON: It is tea still you can make only while there is water.

HENRY: Simon, Simon. A business proposal for you. Money.

I need it up front,
I need it to invest.
I don't have it to hand;
it's all tied up.

SIMON: How much?

HENRY: Don't feel you have to, but you would of course
　　earn interest.

SIMON: (*Louder and clearer – to an old man.*)
　　How much do you want?

HENRY: Ten thousand.

SIMON: Ten!

HENRY: Do you have that much?

SIMON: (*Whisper.*)
　　Just/ I/

　　Pause.

HENRY: Am I worth your salt?
　　I loved you little Sigh-Sigh, dancing
　　mudeater in spiderman-hero pyjamas.
　　I'd wipe your softface up,
　　dried ground downfalling,
　　picks of unsound earth.
　　But we move on.

　　I haven't got long now.

SIMON: Father, I/

HENRY: Simonson.
　　When I die and
　　my teeth are sent down
　　from the sky of my mouth
　　to the skin of the earth,
　　(stone tears biting the dust,)
　　I give you even them.
　　Those failed, fucked little pearls of wisdom.

SIMON: Yes, father. Yes. I/ Wait. When for?

HENRY: As soon as possible. Call. Trans/ Translate it.

SIMON: Transfer it?

HENRY: Yes.

*Exit SIMON. HENRY seems relieved and happy. He takes
the note / drawing from his pocket and thinks out loud.*

SimonDaniel.
How to keep the both you happy?
How to give the both you my all?
It is that I have nothing but what flows through me.But
I'm not saying to Simon *who* it is she loves.
I'll say only that there is someone. That is fair to both,
because fair's fair, Simon. Fair's fair.

*HENRY puts the note / drawing in his pocket. Enter
SIMON.*

SIMON: (*To HENRY – singsong.*)
All done.

Pause.

HENRY: Listen.
Your mother left me one Christmas,
gived me a bloody smear down the night,
a hand all upcut and grazedoff with her
when she pushed and I came down on cheap fairy lights,
pieces of fate earthed on the floor.

And when I fistflexed a few drops felled. Sound like the
roof was all broked up and the rain come in. Sound like
the come of a cry.

HENRY shows SIMON his hand, which carries a scar.

Si – here. Ex marks the spot. (*Beat.*)

And after fighting on Boxing Day
upstairs there a hair slapbang in the bath,
twisted puzzletree confused,
(and I'm blooding bigly now)
is it mine or hers?

But it was him.
But it was his.

I know what it is to love and not to have. And I don't
want this to go round again.

Simon. Look you to your wife.
As a thankyou I tell you.
Do you hold this news;
Miranda is loving another.

SIMON: No. You're wrong.
Never.

HENRY: Simon,
it is always at your side I am.
Never am *I* going from you.

SIMON: When I found her first, she was pissed, playing
badminton.

With an underdraft, a slight giving of air to the door,
it swings and I see her,
smacking new shuttlecocks, featherlight.

She loves me, dad. I was her first.

Have you seen anything?

Pause.

HENRY: No. It is not that I can hold a letter to you and say
'see the real of this'. I/ I have no proof. But as I am old,
look up to me and see that I know, that I just know. And
I am knowing this like I am knowing how to turn a calf
in a cow, how water hides in cactus stems, how to speak
to a child when his mother has left; I am your father and
I am knowing this like those things, I am knowing it.

SIMON: You have no proof. And now you say on me she's/
Is it you are jealous? Do you want me to yourself?
You/

Exit SIMON as HENRY takes the note / drawing from his pocket.

HENRY: (*Shouting.*)
Simon.

Pause. He puts the note / drawing back in his pocket.

(*Shouting.*) Simon, remember the time/

Pause.

Simon, remember/ that sandcastle?

Silence.

To himself.

We landed stars in the sand then.
We stuck poppies to a page then.
Rolling balls in leftover dough
we made shapes in spare time.

So. Simon goes, he does. He goes. He goes off away out in on me.

Shouting.

Don't leave me, don't leave me alone, please don't go.

Silence.

His money to Daniel, then. His money to DanielMiranda.

Scene Eleven

Enter MIRANDA.

MIRANDA: Henry/ I/ I saw your letters. Why you lie on us? You have no money. It is only me and Freyja who know this now, but there is in me the asking of why you hold this to yourself and pretend to have much?

Pause.

HENRY: If SimonDaniel knew
    they would leave me all sunken,
    abrisen with no shoulder to die on.

MIRANDA: Like a child, Henry, you a child like on the
    first day at school;
    'don't leave me, don't go, please stay'. You can't lie on
    your own sons nomore. Can't please both. What if/ What
    if one of them is needing money one time? Can't sudden
    dropquick say it then. (*Beat.*) I am to tell them. I am to
    tell them you have nothing.

HENRY: I love them both. Equally.

MIRANDA: A parental phrase.
    You will be a forgotten thought,
    taken from photographs,
    borrowed nowthen, spoken of by the negatives;
    alone.

HENRY: Hush you up about the letters, hush you up about
    my nothing. Don't tell them. Hush you up, hush you,
    hush. Please. (*Pause.*)

Simon knows.

MIRANDA: What?

HENRY: Simon knows you are not his. I told him. Freyja
    told me. You tell them I have nothing, I'll tell them of
    the time/ Before you met Simon. (*Pause.*) Oh yes, was
    money in all that too. You're knowing all about making
    money, making love. They'll think it's only money
    you'll ever love. Not them.

MIRANDA is defeated.

So don't threaten me.

Or you will not have Simon.

And you will not have Daniel.

Pause.

Stop it with Daniel. It's better to tell Daniel you're not loving him, than me to tell him of your past. (*Beat.*) You really love him? That's what you'd do. That's what you'd do.

I'll tell Simon I was wrong about you. You stop it with Daniel. All will be back as it was.

Beat.

MIRANDA: It may be only a day ago, I was with Daniel. And it might be/ It might be too soon/ But I'm thinking/ I'm thinking I carry him with me.

She puts a hand on her stomach.

MIRANDA moves as though to exit. HENRY catches hold of her.

HENRY: Miranda, I know how it is not to have.
Sometimes in the ache of the moon I think I have seen a little bit of heaven,
a little bit of her.
I have seen it in the two sun loungers,
empty at the yard's end.
White bones bleached by the moon.
Dinosaurs of her day
picked clean, undressed.

I know. I'm knowing.

Exit MIRANDA.

But this is it. How is it that I say 'I lied, Simon, I was wrong and there's no one but you?' Is like to say; 'hate me Simon, and go away off of me', is like to say 'I lied, Simon, for to be having you all to myself and not her', how is it that I say 'I lied' and hold him close still?

Looking at the drawing.

She will end it with him.
She would do it for a song.

I can see it now.

She tells him in his halfsleep
at the turning of the night.
She floats words through milkmist
kissed out at him on a lake.
The words are
ended
no more
gone.
The words are
finished
over
thirsty.
Words whiter than bone.
Words sharper than stone.
All inbreathed.
All inbrothen.
All inbred.
It is art to fly speech in the air.

He blows his body against her
like leaves.
(He knows.)

Pause.

I knew.

There was a woman, I loved her.
There was a woman, I loved her.
There is a woman, I love her.
Still.
As weed out of water.

Very softly; as though naming a child for the first time.

Daniel. Moonlighting son.

Exit HENRY.

Scene Twelve

Enter DANIEL.

DANIEL: Miranda, come on. Longtime I'm here for you,
longtime lovermine.

Enter MIRANDA.

Miranda, soft my sweet.
Freyja's taken the candled Christmas cake out under the
sky.
There's a light flickering in the shed.
The others are shut there.
Go us both now.

Pause.

I love you.

MIRANDA: No. Daniel. Never am I going.

You are in me, spent leadshot, and
I'm not wanting you no more.
You are cross me like train tracks scarve the earth and
I'm not wanting you no more.
You are by me, dull as a twice-read book, and
I'm not wanting you no more.

Silence.

In me there is nothing for you.

DANIEL: This hurting, Miranda.
Is no your heart in it.

MIRANDA: You are in me.
You are cross me.

You are by me.
And I'm not wanting you no more.

DANIEL: I will give you my rubber ball,
    had since I was six.
    I will fill for you my old glow-worm jars,
    the pitch of them starring our roof.
    You will have the taste of me
    stretched over all the time I have known.

    I am loving you, Miranda.
    Is it only a child that you were wanting?

MIRANDA: No! (*Pause.*)

    You are in me, spent leadshot, and
    I'm not wanting you no more.
    You are cross me like train tracks scarve the earth and
    I'm not wanting you no more.
    You are by me, dull as a twice-read book, and
    I'm not wanting you no more.

    DANIEL hits her, hard, across the mouth. Pause. He fingers his own mouth.

DANIEL: I am loving you.

    Pause.

    And I am loving you.

    Pause.

    And I am loving you.
    Until light waves fall to beaches.
    Until leap years stumble home.

    Exit DANIEL. Pause.

MIRANDA: I've been done put a stop to it. Happy Henry?

    Pause.

    Daniel.

Beat.

Still it is that I love him.

I knew him well.
I carry his double;
through him
within,
inside.

His child. (*Pause.*) What is Simon to say? Will be
knowing is not his, is not never his stuff invested here. Is
never that it can be his. Then I will not have Simon. And
I will not have Daniel. *I* will be alone. (*Beat.*) Daniel (?)

Turn your mind to me in nine months
when it is that I am making baby clothes,
when it is like I am stitching shrouds.

Sitting on the porch is night coming in, is.
Is night coming in.
Darkling hand takes the light away,
takes the sight away.
Our pouting white eye-sockets, earthed by the
hauling of the moon, by the
keening of the live, by the
rawling of the sea:
Time taking all our pieces away.

Exit MIRANDA.

Scene Thirteen

Enter SIMON and FREYJA.

FREYJA: Simon. Miranda/ is with/ someone else.

Silence.

I'm sorry.

SIMON: Farth spoke the same.

(*Pause.*) So who is it? He in the city?

Pause.

FREYJA: Henry didn't say?

SIMON: No. Who?

FREYJA: Is Daniel.

SIMON laughs, thinks about this and stops laughing. Silence.

SIMON: I/ I remember. When first we got here. I walked me into/ nothing clear happening. But something. Between them.
Had I not touched and teared her when we slept
Had I not felt and failed her when we touched
Had I not said 'no children' when we feeled
Would it all be alright, then?

FREYJA: Had I not played and loosed him when we fighted
Had I not loved and licked him when we played
Had I not come and missed him when we loved
Would it all be alright, then?

SIMON: (*To himself.*)
Daniel.
Had I not touched and teared you when we slept
Had I not felt and failed you when we touched
Had I not said 'we're children' when we feeled
Would it all be alright, now?

Pause.

FREYJA: Henry knows. I told him. And if it's that he's not telling you, he's helping them.

SIMON: No. No. Never. Farth doesn't know who it is.

FREYJA: Ask him. I told him to talk with Daniel. To help. He didn't. He's with them.

And Miranda says he gave them money, for to leave
with, but he doesn't have any money. (*Beat.*) He doesn't
have any money! Ask him. Then you'll see whose side
he's on. Ask him.

SIMON: (*Shouting.*) Go away, go away.

FREYJA: Ask him.

Exit FREYJA.

SIMON: Daniel. Is this your own back?

My brother.
I know *I* have nothing for her.

Black/exit SIMON.

Scene Fourteen

*DANIEL, outside in the sand. His clothes are dishevelled and
there is blood on them. His flies are undone. He is barefoot. He
is drunk and holds a half-empty bottle and a huge wad of
(unidentifiable) money and a box of matches. He sits and mutters
to himself whilst drawing a circle around himself in the sand.
He lays the money around him in a circle in a way suggestive of
the way HENRY lays out the photographs in the next scene. He
takes a pebble from the sand and, closing his eyes, he stands in
the circle and turns around to lose his bearings. Then he crouches
down and hides the pebble under a note. He stands again, spins
again, and sits.*

DANIEL: Go ahead. Choose.

*Beat. He points to a note. He lifts the note, but the pebble
is not there.*

Bad luck.
I'll take this.
What do you need it for now?

With the matches he burns the note.

Give it another go.

Again he points to another note. He lifts the note, but the pebble is not there.

Never mind.
If at first you don't succeed…

With the matches he burns the note.

And again.

Again he points to a note. He lifts the note, but the pebble is not there.

Not very good at this, are you? Useless waste.

With the matches he burns every other note in the circle, prodding the ashes to see if the pebble is there. It is not.

He burns every third note there. He finds the pebble and kisses it, then throws it off into the sand. He takes a swig of drink, pushes all the remaining notes together and burns them.

Blackout.

Scene Fifteen

Inside. Enter HENRY with a heavy photograph album, several pictures spilling out. They fall from his hands and he drops the album.

HENRY: Ah. Stupid. Stupid old person you.

He begins sorting the photographs into piles around him. They encircle him completely.

Simon. Simon. Simon-Daniel. Daniel-Simon. Daniel-Simon-me. Daniel. Daniel. Daniel. Daniel. Daniel-Freyja wedding. Simon-Miranda wedding. Simon and rabbit. (Seventh birthday present.)

I am going on getting on,
but always looking back.
Is as like a child, colouring in,
has fistpressed on my herenow and drawn me down long,
smudged, across time; (*Referring to photographs.*)
Technicolor, Technicolor, Technicolor.
Blackwhite. Blackwhite.
Nothing.

Pause.

And sitting here now I'm looking to my hand.
(What held Daniel's on his first day at school,
what touched her breast, the nipple framed in the fuck of
my fingers,
what played Bach at our wedding, could stretch a
thirteenth,
what pulled triggers on wolves, could drop death from a
distance,
what's waved and woven,
what's punched and driven,
what's fed me,
what's wiped me,
what's scratched me,
what's wanked me.)

Christ; life – I had a hand in it all.

Pause. He takes the drawing/note from his pocket, and looks at it.

SIMON: (*Off.*) Farth?

HENRY holds the writing/paper, hand splayed, against his chest, almost intending SIMON to see it. Enter SIMON.

Farth, I've come to say goodbye. I'm going away off to the mountains. I have been thinking on what you said and now am I with you in it. I can't stay. Knowing she is not mine. I'm sorry I didn't believe you.

HENRY: No, Simon/

SIMON: /Mountains minted greenwhite,
    lines of snow calling us high.
    Warmed curves,
    suckling the sky.

    Always have they called me.
    In the mountains I'll have what I want.

    If I were a bull,
    someone would buy me
    and feed me and kill me.
    And lay out my skin
    and take me to market.
    A young woman would buy me
    and beat me and dry me
    and I would pass the night over
    her body and under
    her body and to the sides of
    her body.
    The break of pelt on skin.
    Her man would say
    'It is hide. It is dead.',
    but in the mountains
    I would have her love.

    Pause.

HENRY: Simon/

SIMON: /Is there something you have to say, farth?

    Beat.

HENRY: Don't go. (*Pause.*) Simon. You're not knowing yet for sure.

SIMON: You want me to live with her while she loves another? *You're* knowing why I never could do that.

    Pause.

HENRY: Is not/ Don't go/ Do not you go letting yourself
sprint away, as to say 'I'm shamed, I give you up'.

Listen hard.
Your wife. She loves you.

Silence.

SIMON: Is not what you were saying on me earlier.

HENRY: I/ I was wrong.
Do you love me, Simon?
Do you love me more than your mother?

SIMON: (*Touching him.*)
I love you more than Daniel.

Pause.

HENRY: Listen me/

SIMON: /why before you saying she don't love me no
more? Tell the truth, farth.

HENRY: It's/

SIMON: No! Tell the truth.

Pause.

HENRY: Listen. Don't scrabble for her.

It's like/
I saw a swan this morning, woozywhite in a field of mist.
Let me touch her, tried to hold her
and she cut the clouds, was feeled and missed.
You'll scare her like that.

We *see* nothing done.
We have no hard proof.
Miranda loves you.
Is best to watch and wait and/ and *see*, Simon.
And *see*.

SIMON: Farth. I/ I/ Where the money I lent you? Give it you back me.

Pause.

HENRY: I/

SIMON: Only then will I know who you're with.

Farth.

Pause.

My wife. My brother.

Pause.

SIMON sees the paper which HENRY holds. HENRY freezes. SIMON approaches HENRY. He prises HENRY's fingers up and takes the drawing/note.

Why weren't you showing me this? It's with Daniel you are.

HENRY: No. I/ I couldn't tell you. I didn't tell you was Daniel to save you knowing that. To/ to spare you/

SIMON: /And this is loving me
like the me you loved age thirteen,
when you beat me with a belt.

Is loving me like the sad love drink.
Is loving me like the fat love food.

Pause. HENRY tries to think of a way to comfort SIMON.

HENRY: Pass me the note.

SIMON passes the writing/note to HENRY.

SIMON: Farth, you have to hear this. When Dan was twelve and/ there was something happened/

HENRY: (*Looking at the writing / note.*)
/This not recent, Si/ I/ Is maybe just once what was months before.

Pause.

Your wife. She loves you.
They come back you see.

SIMON: Do they?

Pause.

HENRY: Give me a chance Simon. (*Beat.*) Don't judge me
   yet. I will get your silver. I am not with Daniel.

SIMON sits/lies down.

SIMON: What's the truth?
   When I was young I knew.

   Return my money. Then I'll know who you're with.

SIMON grows tired during the following.

HENRY: Remember the geery evening spooled small,
   wound round the smacking of the stabledoor,
   only the smacking of the stabledoor,
   just the smacking of the stabledoor
   and the snatching of my staplegun
   biting paper,
   beating time.
   Simple time;
   stupid time.
   And a cat pausing.
   Full doobies swinging.
   Worrying when to drop her litter;
   having kittens.
   Listening with her cat's whisker
   to the smacking of the stabledoor
   only the smacking of the stabledoor
   just the smacking of the stabledoor.

   I remember the space in those beats,
   the spaces between us then.

There are people we love that we never touch.
And hard is the downbeat of days.

You will have your money.

Pause.

Goodnight Simon. I will get your money.
(*Aside.*) May sight of the silver stay you to your home.

SIMON sleeps.

Scene Sixteen

Enter DANIEL, drunk. HENRY talks quieter than DANIEL throughout – trying not to wake SIMON. DANIEL is not concerned at the prospect of SIMON waking.

DANIEL: Hello. I'm back my farth, sweet my dearie.

HENRY: Hush you.

DANIEL: And what time do I call this?? All time and no time, sweetie pie, all time and no time.

HENRY: You lied.

Pause.

The money was for you-Miranda to run away with.
Never for no specialist. There's nothing wrong with you.

Silence.

DANIEL: She whispered me
'meet me at the holdingplace, back of the shed'.
So I did.
She runned in
with wet grass,
green ribbons
screaming 'go' down her back.

And then she said.

You are in me, spent leadshot, and
I'm not wanting you no more.
You are cross me like train tracks scarve the earth and
I'm not wanting you no more.
You are by me, dull as a twice-read book, and
I'm not wanting you no more.

Pause.

Now, now, oh yes, I am seeing who put her up to it. Our
father, it is *yours* the glory, the kingdom and the power.

Silence.

HENRY: I'm not wanting to see it all fall round again.
What happened to me and her. You can still be happy
with Freyja.

Pause.

I want to spare you.

DANIEL: Thanks.

Tomorrow am I going.
If still you can 'spare' me.
Think of the oftentimes when small I was
and taked I a sandwich, some water,
and sitted on the wall outside and wouldn't
never come back in. Called it leaving home.
You called it growing up.
But there wasn't no where to leave to.
Was only the sandskin.
And I walked me out on the desert,
walked me over the poor grains, the hot wastes,
for the green mountains.
But you came after me.
Said

HENRY: I love you

DANIEL: like a handclamp to the shoulder.
  Said

HENRY: I'm sorry

DANIEL: like man to woman.
  Said

HENRY: get in.

DANIEL: And always I did.

  But not this time.
  There's nothing here for me.
  Tomorrow am I going.
  If still you can 'spare' me.

HENRY: Daniel. Where's the money?

  Pause.

DANIEL: Why? You've got money to burn.
  It is nothing to you, what I borrowed.
  You have the richness of rain on ground,
  of a child's kiss,
  of fois-gras.
  You have the strength of lightening,
  of a parent's hand,
  of a king,
  of dad.
  Live forever.

  Pause.

  (*Quietly.*) When I was twelve/ When was I twelve/

  Pause.

  When I was and Simon took me,
  I told you.
  You stopped your eyes.
  And you holded my name like a doll

that still you don't know what to do with.
Simple straight pure
and teddybear-close.
Innocence is in me.

Pause.

You're not needing the money.
And I don't have it.
Is spent like seeds on the sand.
Where only the heat will rise.

So what time do I call this, then? All time and no time. I
leave you as I come.

DANIEL moves to leave.

HENRY: (*Shouting.*) Daniel!

*In the shadows DANIEL hesitates and turns. SIMON is
woken by HENRY's shout. He does not see DANIEL.*

Scene Seventeen

HENRY: (*Quietly.*) Simon.

Pause.

Simon.

SIMON: Farth?

HENRY: Hush you now, hush you.

SIMON: What's up?

HENRY: Simon.

Silence.

Remember. You held the age of five.
And Baron, he went swallowed rat poison,
closed his mouth around his death,

bit off more than he could chew.
And then you said on me

SIMON: make him stand

HENRY: and

SIMON: make him move

HENRY: and

SIMON: make him be to me Baron again.
Is only *playing* dead.

Pause.

HENRY: But I was not having it in me to do that.

Pause.

And just like that, and just like that I don't have your silver.

Silence.

SIMON: Why?

Silence.

DANIEL: He doesn't have it because he gave it to me. And I burnt it.

Pause.

And it's in me that if he can't pay now, he has no more. (*Sing-song.*) Liar, liar his pants is on fire.

Silence.

SIMON: Daniel. It was that you and Miranda were wanting the money?

Pause.

DANIEL: Yes.

Silence.

In the darkening of her
there is growing my child.
What never would you give her.

HENRY: (*To DANIEL.*) You can't *know* that. (*To SIMON.*) It's
what she says.

Silence.

SIMON: Miranda.
First-one.
A trapdoor spider;
(won't you come into my parlour?)
Deeds of darkness
up in arms.
Farth, you/ I told you if you couldn't get the money/
You're with him. Liar. I'm going. I'm going to the
mountains. (*Pause.*)

Leave me. Leave me.

Exit HENRY.

DANIEL: Simon. (*Pause.*) Sorry.

Simon?

SIMON: She loves you.

Pause.

DANIEL: No.
Is a child, is a child she's wanting.
Is a child she's begging for.

SIMON: Is more.

DANIEL: What?

SIMON: Is more to why you took her.

Silence.

Daniel? Is this your own back? Is it that, is it the thing
that when the river died, river died we were small, is it
then playing in the mud, stickinthemud, mud wet,
muddled, rolling in it, is it then, the thing there was then,
thing there was then happened. (*Pause.*) Thing I did to
you?

DANIEL: Everything was of gold then.
　　　The sand, the sun.
　　　And in the backing was the mountains,
　　　green taps on the shoulder saying

DANIEL / SIMON: (*SIMON putting his hand on DANIEL's
　　　shoulder from behind – their bodies are close against each
　　　other, suggesting the positions of their childhood selves that
　　　night.*) I'm here.

　　　DANIEL stiffens but does not turn round. Silence.

SIMON: Tag
　　　Mudstick
　　　Kisschase
　　　Families
　　　Childblood playing with knives and fire.
　　　Ip dip boys' screams falling from the sky
　　　to the cuffs of the adult.
　　　I'm sorry.

DANIEL: I let you.

SIMON: You were twelve.

DANIEL: (*So?*) You were only thirteen.

　　　Pause.

SIMON: Did I hurt you?

DANIEL: No.

　　　Pause.

　　　Yes.

Pause.

I was twelve. (*Explanation for the pain.*)

SIMON: I was only thirteen.

Silence. Silence.

DANIEL: Simon. I went back to my room after. Same room
    I have again. I see
    moon is fatty,
    farplaced, foreign.

SIMON approaches him.

Stand you off away out in on me.
It was this room, my room.
A Constable cried down the wall.
Sour grass. Dogroses. Fuckedup buttercups.
Forked trees; vulvas
sticking the sky.
A shyer horse,
wearing his neigh round his ankles.
Childblood screams and plays in
side of the moon.

SIMON: (*SIMON approaches him.*) Daniel, I/

DANIEL: Listen you, always far from me.

SIMON reaches out.

Stand you off away out in on me.
Is all hard as stone,
is all arm's length all ways.

SIMON: Daniel/

DANIEL: With Miranda is as something softreaches me
    and I do then get be thinking
    yes, wish as is now I could give her me.
    Open up like a cabinet.

Take my PeterPan off.
Shine straight as
sun in the sky.
No. Is always you,
is always that night, and
I'm hided

SIMON: to cry. (*Approaching DANIEL successfully.*)
Cry, softbrother.
That night was one star cried down the sky and
we lay, watched the dancings.

DANIEL: One star there was,

SIMON: one star,

DANIEL: pushing through the night.
Like lead pipe in earth.

SIMON: Like an arrow on a blackboard saying

DANIEL: here

SIMON: here

DANIEL: here

SIMON: here

DANIEL: here.

Silence. They kiss on the lips. After a beat or two DANIEL pushes SIMON away. Pause.

Good night.

Exit DANIEL.

SIMON: (*Shouting.*) Daniel? (*Pause.*) Daniel!
(*Not shouted.*)
Daniel, what's to be?
What's over the hills for us,
what's under the streets for us,

81

what's down the alley's dark gut?
(*Sing-song.*) All gone.
My money.
My wife.
My father.
My life.

*Long silence. SIMON strips naked and then dresses in
his pyjamas. They are suggestive of a child's pyjamas. He
does not speak until fully clothed.*

Miranda.
Scattered.
Hair on the pillow
like pollen knocked up by rain.
Her on the pillow
like pollen gone down again.
And when the case is stripped
see the stained worlds she spoke in silence in spit in
sleep,
those mindless Midas marks.
Miranda.
Hair on the pillow.
Her on the pill,
low as a whore,
her on the pull.
Death waits at the kissing gate
and I am touched by a feral star.

There was a woman, I loved her.
There was a woman, I loved her.
There is a woman, I love her.
Still.

As weed out of water.
Tag
Mudstick
Kisschase

Families
Childblood playing with knives and fire/

He hangs himself. The shadow of his body is cast over the Monopoly board. Darkness.

Scene Eighteen

Light. The pyjamas SIMON wore are on a coathanger, positioned where he hanged himself. Enter HENRY, who busies himself for some time, managing to avoid looking at them. Eventually he stands in front of them, looking at the floor in silence.

HENRY: Simon. First-born.
   (*Flatly.*) Don't leave me.

Silence. Enter DANIEL. He carries a bag. HENRY does not acknowledge DANIEL; he speaks to the pyjamas.

(*Sing-song.*) All gone.
Simon.

Fingering the pyjamas, brushing them against his cheek – a motion suggestive of his earlier caressing of Sarah's letters. Very introverted and flat.

I touch the rags of a son to me,
a symmetry made from reeltoreel thread soft as guts.
Simon. I see my splayed hand, I hold you hardly.

Silence. He extends his hand towards the pyjamas, which hang above him. As he is about to touch them, he turns this movement into a swift brushing motion on the shoulders. He stops. The arm of the pyjamas falls about his shoulders. HENRY still does not acknowledge DANIEL, but addresses the pyjamas.

Remember.
On the plain walked we once
and you said

DANIEL: is where, the pure green land?

HENRY: As a child you wondered
   who rolled the moon
   and stretched him thin.
   On the plain walked we once
   and you said

DANIEL: is where, the wet blue sea?

HENRY: As a child you wondered
   where tears are made
   and held inside us.

   Pause.

   On the plain walked we once.
   You found a cockle in the sand.
   I watched, mouth open.
   Shellshocked.

   Enter FREYJA.

FREYJA: Henry, we all are going now. Miranda/ won't
   come in.

   Silence.

   To the city. Henry?

   Silence.

   Can't/ can't leave you here.

   Pause.

   Henry! Only is there water for a few days now.

   Silence.

HENRY: (*Without moving.*) Are you leaving him?

FREYJA: I/

HENRY: *Are* you? Leaving him?

*Pause. FREYJA glances to DANIEL. DANIEL remains
impassive.*

FREYJA: No.

Pause.

I am loving him.

Pause.

And I am loving him.

Pause.

And I am loving him.
Until light waves fall to beaches.
Until leap years stumble home.

Silence.

HENRY: I am staying. Is all I've been knowing, this. And I
am been knowing the land like my body. This scar; a
window pane, age twenty-six. This bruise; a gate, last
week. And I am been knowing the land like that. The
shed, Sarah. The barn, sweat.

This is where
This is where I lived
This is where I lived with.
Her.
She might come back.

Pause.

FREYJA: Then. 'Bye Henry.

HENRY: Wait.

FREYJA pauses.

I am sorry.
And tell Miranda, I said nothing.
Tell her I never will.

Exit FREYJA.

Long silence. DANIEL moves as if to exit.

Don't go Daniel.
I want to talk you about books and games.
I want to talk you about scum and stars.
I want to talk you about why children cry with bodies and legs
but adults with just eyes.
What hath God wrought?

Pause.

What hath God wrought?

Pause. DANIEL approaches HENRY.

DANIEL: Our child.

Pause.

Good bye dad.

Exit DANIEL.

HENRY: (*Shouting.*) Daniel!

He listens.

Daniel!

He listens.

I love you.

Pause.

I'm sorry.

Pause. Angry.

Daniel, get in here! (*Pause.*) Now!

He gives up. He cries. He sees the Monopoly board.

Daniel, it's your turn.

Silence. Darkness.

Scene Nineteen

HENRY sits in his chair, as in Scene One. He does not hold the stick / staff. The Monopoly board, still mid-game, remains on the floor. He audibly taps the following in Morse code: (. . . - - - . . .) (S.O.S.) on the arm of his chair. Light fades steadily over the following, to conclude in darkness.

HENRY: Once we were at the zoo,
　　and there was the rain, was.
　　SimonDaniel cracked open their small mouths
　　and laughed wet red calls
　　like cherries into the air.
　　There was the rain, was.
　　There was the rain.
　　Maybe is left at the zoo.

He selects one of his photographic relics and addresses it.

Sarah. Drunk and crying here. You have on your undereye evenings.

(*Calling.*) Daniel. (*Pause.*) Daniel. (*Pause.*) Daniel.

He listens.

Daniel, mine. Been and gone.

(*Calling.*) Simon. Simple skyman, earthed. Come back.

Silence.

Pause. Gabbled. Losing control over his mouth.

Do you know how to craft, do you know how to listen,
do you know how to fight, do you know how to answer,
do you know how to save, do you know how to give up,
do you know how to kill, to slaughter?

Silence.

Sarah, hurry and come.
Sometimes I kiss my bruises well and
I imagine it's you, kissing the blue. (*Pause.*)
The rain is over now.
I remember when you fell asleep
and my fingers dripped with liquid myrrh and
I would mourn your little death;
a wake in the black.
Sarah, slip your voice over the hills.
I'm wandering in the muckie of your smell.

He looks again at the photograph while he speaks the following. Progressively breathless, restless – but he does not touch himself. He is predominantly crying, but with a sense of coming.

I'm hardup without you.
Turn down the cover of night.
Kiss me/
There/
Not too/
Not too dry but rather/
Like a wide-eyed child.
(Kiss me. Better.)

Hold.

Looking on you now
what a catch;

Hold. He comes. The photograph falls from his hands onto the Monopoly board. Then, relaxing;

I win.

The End.